FOOD	Wt. GRAMS	MEASURE	PRO. gms.	FAT gms.	CHO. gms.	CALORIES	Ca. gms.	P. gms.	Fe. mgms.	VITAMINS A	VITAMINS B	VITAMINS C	EXCESS Acid	EXCESS Base	FIBER gms.	WATER gms.	SOURCE	SOURCE
Almonds	100	¾c or 107	21.0	54.9	17.3	647	.239	.465	4.07	+	++	•		12.0	2.0	4.8	A	B1
Apples, fresh	100	2/3 of 2¼" diam, or 1, 2" diam.	.3	.4	13.9	60	.007	.012	.36	+	+	++[5]		3.7	1.0	84.1	C	A
Apple sauce	100	⅜c	.4	.5	30.1	124	.009	.015	.37	•	•	—To+		4.5	1.2		M	
Apricots, fresh,[a7]	100	2, 1⅝" diam.	1.0	.1	12.3	54	.014	.025	.61					6.4	.6	85.4	C	A
Apricots, dried	100	½c packed or 16 small halves	4.7	1.0	60.1	268	.066	.117	7.61					31.3	2.4	29.4	G	A
Apricots, dried, cooked	100	1/3c	1.3		30.7	128	.018	.032	2.01					8.5	.7		M	
Artichokes, globe	200	One 3" diam. 4" long	5.8	.8	17.4[6b]	100			.95	++	+	•			6.4	167.4	D	A
Artichokes, jerusalem,	100		2.2	.1	16.2[6b]	74									.8	79.5	D	
Asparagus, fresh	100	12 5-inch stalks	2.2	.2	3.2	24	.025	.039	.96	++[7]	+++	•		.8	.7	93.0	D	A
Avocado (Alligator Pear)	200	One 4" long	4.0	46.4	13.4	487			.57	++	++	•			2.3	133.4	C	A
Bacon, uncooked	100	10 slices 1½"x4½"x⅛"	10.5	64.8	....	625	.006	.108	1.30	—To+	+	•	5.0			20.2	A	C
Bacon, cooked	15	4 strips 3¼" long	2.5	7.5	....	77	.001[2]	.026[3]	.30[3]	—To+	+	•	1.5				P	C
Bananas	100	One 6½" long or ¾c. sliced	1.2	.2	22.4	96	.009	.031	.64	+To++	+	++		5.6	.6	74.8	C	A
Barley, pearled	100	½c	8.5	1.1	77.8	355	.043	.400	3.58	•	++	•	10.4		.3	11.5	A	B1
Beansprouts, Mung	100	+½c	2.9	.3	3.3	27				+	++	++ Cooked +++ Raw			.7	92.4	D	
Beans, kidney, canned	100	½c	7.0	.2	17.3	99	.043[2]	.158[3]	2.31[2]	•	•	—		3.0	1.2	72.7	A	B1
Beans, navy, dried	100	½c	22.5	1.8	55.2	327	.160	.471	7.93	•	++	•		18.0	4.4	12.6	A	A
Beans, baked, canned	100	½c	6.9	2.5	17.1	118	.042	.340	2.05	+	++	•		6.4	1.3	68.9	A	H
Beans, soy, dried or meal	100	½c	36.7	18.2	26.6	417	.206	.580	.78	+	++	—			5.1	8.0	R	A
Bean, soy, green, shelled	100	+½c	12.4	6.3	12.2[8]	155	.079	.222	.3	+	++	•			2.2	64.7	R	
Beans, snap, raw	100	2/3c	2.4	.2	6.3	37	.046	.052	.98	++	++	++		5.4	1.4	88.9	D	A

Pro. Protein
CHO. Carbohydrate (total, excluding fiber)
Ca. Calcium
P. Phosphorus
Fe. Iron

The percentage composition of fruits and vegtables is that of raw food.

Excess Acid or Base expressed as cc. Normal solution required to neutralize the ashed food
Source See pp. 17

Vitamins
— No appreciable content
\+ Food contains the vitamin
++ A good source
+++ An excellent source
• Evidence is doubtful or insufficient
Var. Variable

Vitamin D
\+ Green leafy vegetables
++ Milk, cream, butter, egg yolk
+++ Cod liver oil

Vitamin E
\+ Milk, muscle meat, egg yolk
+++ Wheat embryo, lettuce

E.P. Edible Portion. Analysis given in E.P. unless otherwise noted.
A.P. As purchased
c Cupful (standard 8 oz.)
" Inches
T. Tablespoonful
t. teaspoonful

1 Includes fiber
2 Calculated from dried food
3 Calculated from uncooked food
4 Acid ash due to benzoic acid content
5 Storage apples Vit. C +
5a Presumably a considerable proportion of inulin
6b Much of this is inulin
7 Bleached Vit. A —
8 About 5% is available

FOOD	Wt. GRAMS	MEASURE	PRO. gms.	FAT gms.	CHO. gms.	CALORIES	Ca. gms.	P. gms.	Fe. mgms.	VITAMINS A	VITAMINS B	VITAMINS C	EXCESS Acid	EXCESS Base	FIBER gms.	WATER gms.	SOURCE	
Beans, lima, green, shelled	100	½c	7.5	.8	22.0	125	.028	.133	2.40					14.0	1.5	66.5	D	A
Beans, lima, dried	100	2/3c	18.1	1.5	65.9[3]	349	.071	.338	8.62					41.6		10.4	A	A
Beef bouillon	100	—½c	2.2	.1	.2	18										96.6	A	
Beef, misc. fat free cuts	100	4"x4"x½"	22.4	2.9		116	.013	.241	4.1	+	+	—To+	11.5			73.8	A	B_1
Beef, round, lean	100	4"x4"x½"	19.7	8.0		151	.011	.212	4.1	+	+	—To+	10.6			71.0	B	B_1
Beef, loin, med. fat	100	4"x4"x½"	16.9	25.0		293	.010	.182	3.7	+	+	—To+	10.8			57.0	B	B_1
Beef, loin, fat	100	4"x4"x½"	15.6	31.0		341	.009	.168	3.7	+	+	—To+	9.5			53.0	B	B_1
Beef, roast, fat	100	1 slice 5"x2½"x¼"	22.3	28.6		347	.013	.240	4.9[3]	+	+	—To+	11.7			48.2	A	B_1
Beef, dried	100	7 slices 4"x5"	30.0	6.5		178	.017	.323	6.2[3]				14.8			54.3	A	B_1
Beef, dried, creamed	100	½c	8.0	10.9	7.1	158	.090	.125	1.26				1.6				M	(2)
Beef, stew with vegetables	100	½c	5.3	4.6	12.9	114	.022	.080	1.58					2.0	.4		M	
Beef, juice	100	½c	4.9	.6		25	.008	.031	44.4	•	+	—To+	2.4			93.0	A	C
Beer 3.5% alcohol or less	100		.4		3.8	39											S	
Beer 3.5% alcohol or less	12 oz	1 bottle	1.4		13.0	133											S	
Beer 3.5-6% alcohol	100		.6		4.7	51											S	
Beer 3.5-6% alcohol	12 oz	1 bottle	2.0		16.0	173											S	
Ale 6% alcohol or more	100		.7		4.8	72											S	
Ale 6% alcohol or more	12 oz	1 bottle	2.4		16.0	245											S	
Beet greens	100	½c cooked	2.0	.3	4.2	27			3.13	++	++	•		27.0[9]	1.4	90.4	D	A
Beets	100	½c diced	1.6	.1	8.7	41	.029	.039	.85	—To+	+	+		10.9	.9	87.6	D	A
Biscuit, Baking Powder	35	2 small Biscuits	2.5	2.9	14.4	94	.022	.031	.20				1.5				M	
Blackberries, fresh[37]	100	1 1/6c	1.2	1.1	7.8	46	.017	.034	.91						4.1	85.3	C	A
Blueberries[37]	100	2/3c	.6	.6	13.9	63	.020	.008	.80						1.2	83.4	C	A
Bologna	30	4"x4"x⅛"	5.6	5.3	.1	70	.001	.018	.84				2.8			18.0	A	D
Bran	100	2c unwashed	16.4	6.1	12.2[10]	169	.120	1.215	8.52	+	++	—			6.0	6.0	L	B_1
Brazil-nuts	100		16.8	69.4	5.0	712			3.93	+	++	•			2.1	5.3	L	B_1

[9] No data available. Value given is that of spinach.
[10] An additional 46.9% is quoted as undetermined carbohydrate.

FOOD	WT. GRAMS	MEASURE	PRO. gms.	FAT gms.	CHO. gms.	CALORIES	Ca. gms.	P. gms.	Fe. mgms.	VITAMINS A	VITAMINS B	VITAMINS C	EXCESS Acid	EXCESS Base	FIBER gms.	WATER gms.	SOURCE
Bread, graham	100	3 1/3 slices - 3/8"	8.9	1.8	51.0	256	.050	.218	2.5	+	++	—	6.8		1.1	35.7	A D
Bread, graham	30	1 slice	2.7	.5	15.3	77	.015	.065	.7	+	++	—	2.0		.3	10.7	A D
Bread, rye	100	3 1/3 slices - 3/8"	9.0	.6	52.7	252	.024	.148	1.6	*	++	*	6.8		.5	35.7	A D
Bread, rye	30	1 slice	2.7	.2	15.8	76	.007	.044	.5	*	++	*			.1	10.7	A D
Bread, white (milk)	100	3 1/3 slices - 3/8"	9.6	1.4	31.1	255				+	+	—To+	7.1			36.5	A A
Bread, white (milk)	30	1 slice	2.9	.4	15.3	76				+	+	—To+	2.1			10.9	A A
Bread, white (water)	100	3 1/3 slices - 3/8"	9.3	1.2	52.2	257	.027	.093	.9	*	+	—	7.1		.5	35.6	A D
Bread, white (water)	30	1 slice	2.8	.4	15.7	77	.008	.028	.3	*	+	—	2.1		.1	10.7	A D
Bread, whole wheat	100	3 1/3 slices - 3/8"	9.7	.9	48.5	241	.05	.175	1.6	Milk++ Water+	++ ++	—To+ —	7.3		1.2	38.4	A D
Bread, whole wheat	30	1 slice	2.9	.3	14.6	72	.015	.052	.5	See above			2.2		.4	11.5	A D
Broccoli	100	2 5" stalks	3.3	.2	4.2	32		Buds 1.42 Leaves 1.38							1.3	89.9	D A
Butter	100	7T	1.0	85.0		769	.015	.017	.2	+++	—	*		Neutral		11.0	A D
Butter	10	1 square 1¼"x1¼"x¼"	.1	8.5		77	.001	.002	.02	+++	—	*		Neutral		1.1	A D
Butter	14	1T	.1	11.9		108	.002	.002	.03	+++	—	*		Neutral		1.5	A D
Butter	226	1c	2.3	192.1		1738	.034	.038	.45	+++	—	*		Neutral		24.9	A D
Buttermilk (churned)	100	½c	3.0	.5	4.8	36	.105	.097	.25	+	++	—To+		2.2		91.0	A D
Butternuts	100	25 nuts	27.9	61.2	3.5[1]	676			6.84	+	++	*	6.84			4.4	A B₁
Brussels sprouts	100	2/3c	4.4	.5	7.6	52	.027	.120	1.17	*	++			6.0[15]	1.3	84.9	D A
Cabbage Chinese	100	3/4c shredded	1.4	.1	1.8	14			.62	*	*	++			.6	95.2	D A
Cabbage, white, fresh	100	2/3c cooked; 1½c raw	1.4	.2	4.3	25	.045	.029	.43 green 1.22 rhd 1.04	+	++	+++		6.0	1.0	92.4	D A
Cake, plain	56	2½"x2½"x1¾"	3.7	7.4	29.3	199	.027	.045	.39				2.4				M
Cake, chocolate	50	2½"x2½"x1¾"	3.0	9.3	24.0	191	.021	.048	.40				1.8				M
Cantelopes, E.P.	100	½c pulp: 1/3 of 4½" melon	.6	.2	5.1	25	.017	.013	.39	++	++	++		7.5	.7	92.8	C A
Carrots	100	¾c cooked	1.2	.3	8.2	40	.056	.046	.64	+++	++	+To++		10.8	1.1	88.2	D A

* No data available. Figure given is that of cabbage.

FOOD	Wt. GRAMS	MEASURE	PRO. gms.	FAT gms.	CHO. gms.	CALORIES	Ca. gms.	P. gms.	Fe. mgms.	VITAMINS A	VITAMINS B	VITAMINS C	EXCESS Acid	EXCESS Base	FIBER gms.	WATER gms.	SOURCE	
Cauliflower	100	2/3c cooked	2.4	.2	4.0	27	.123	.061	.94	•	+To++	•		5.3	.9	91.7	D	A
Celery	100	4 Med. Stalks or ¾c cut	1.3	.2	3.0	19	.078	.037	.62	-To+	++	•		7.8	.7	91.7	D	A
Chard (leaves only)	100	1/3c cooked	2.6	.4	4.0	28	.150	.040	3.09	++	+To++	•		15.7	.8	91.0	D	E
Cheese, cheddar (American)	100	3"x2"x1" or ¾c grated	27.7	36.8	4.1	458	.931	.683	1.38	++	*	•	5.5			27.4	A	A
Cheese, cottage, skim	100	½c or 6 T	20.9	1.0	4.3	110	.077			*	*	•				72.0	A	F
Cherries, sour,"	100	2/3c	1.3	.5	13.0	62	.019	.031	red .41	++	++	•		6.1	.3	84.4	H	A
Cherries, sweet,"	100	2/3c	1.1	.5	17.4	78	.019	.031	black .77	++	++	•			.4	80.0	C	A
Chestnuts	100		6.2	5.4	40.3	235	.034	.093	4.10	•	+	•		7.6	1.8	45.0	A	B₁
Chicken, broilers, E.P.	100	½ med. size	21.5	2.5		108	.012	.232	.70[10]	-To+	+	•	10.8			74.8	A	B₁
Chicken, fowl, uncooked	70[11]	½ breast or one thigh	19.3	16.3		224	.011	.208	Light meat .70[10]	-To+	+	•	9.6			63.7	A	B₁
Chicken, fowl, stewed	70	½ breast or one thigh	19.3	14.3		206	....	....	Dark meat 1.01	-To+	+	•	9.6				A	B₁
Chicken salad	70	¾c + 2 leaves lettuce	4.6	11.9	1.1	130	.025	.061	.39			•	.7		.2		M	
Chicory	100		1.6	.3	2.1	17			.49			•			.8	94.2	D	A
Chocolate, bitter	100	3 1/3 squares	12.9	48.7	30.3[12]	611	.092	.455	3.15	-	*	•				5.9	A	B₁
Chocolate, bitter	28	1 square	3.6	13.6	8.5[12]	171	.026	.127	.88	-	*	•				1.8	A	B₁
Chocolate, milk, bar	60	bar 6½"x3"x3/16"	4.8	21.0	30.7	331											F	
Chocolate blanc mange	100	½c	3.5	6.6	26.3	179	.102	.106	.41					1.4			M	
Citron	100	1¼c sliced	.5	1.5	78.1[12]	328	.121	.033		-				9.7		19.0	A	B₁
Cocoa, dry	100	5/6 c	21.6	28.9	37.7	497	.112	.709	2.7			•				4.6	A	B₁
Cocoa	2.5	1t	.5	.7	.9[12]	12	.003	.018	.08							.1	A	B₁
Cocoa	7.5	1T	1.6	2.2	2.8	37	.009	.054	.23							.3	A	B₁
Cocoa, beverage	100	2/3c	6.0	7.3	14.9	148	.195	.172	.48					2.9			M	(a)
Cocoanut, shredded	170	5 4/5c	6.3	57.4	31.5[12]	668	.059	.135	2.67	+	++			7.1		3.5	A	B₁
Cod, fresh	100	4"x1½"x1"	16.5	.4		70	.018	.192	.34	-To+	+	•	5.5			82.6	A	B₁
Codfish, salt, uncooked	100	piece 4½"x2¾"x½"	25.4	.3		104	.028	.292	.52[10]			•	12.6			53.5	A	B₁

[10] Figure that of Chicken, light meat.
[11] Calculated from Cod, fresh.
[12] Compiler's determination.

FOOD	WT. GRAMS	MEASURE	PRO. gms.	FAT gms.	CHO. gms.	CALORIES	Ca. gms.	P. gms.	Fe. mgms.	VITAMINS A	VITAMINS B	VITAMINS C	EXCESS Acid	EXCESS Base	FIBER gms.	WATER gms.	SOURCE	SOURCE
Codfish, salt, cooked	60ᵃ	1/3c flaked	25.4	.3		104							12.6				A	A
Cod liver oil	14	1 T		14.0		126				+++	—	—					F	A
Chocolate drop cookies	16	1 cooked 2¼" diam.	1.2	3.7	6.5	65	.008	.022	.17				.6				M	
Cookies, sugar (plain)	12	1, 2¼" diam.	.7	1.8	7.0	47	.003	.007	.07				.5				M	
Corn, sweet	100	¾c cooked	3.7	1.1	21.9	102	.006	.103	.47	+	++	—	1.8	.9	72.4	D	A
Corncake (Johnny cake)	34	2"x2"x1"	2.6	3.0	16.0	101	.025	.044	.31				1.4			M	
Cornflakes	100	3½c	8.2	.4	86.7	383	.018	.190	2.78				5.4	.2		F	B₁
Cornflakes	20	2/3c	1.6	.1	17.3	77	.004	.038	.5				1.1			F	B₁
Corn meal, yellow, unckd.	100	2/3c	7.5	4.2	65.9¹	331	.018	.190	1.30	++	++	—	5.4		10.3	A	B₁
Corn meal, cooked	100	1/3c	1.5	.4	12.5¹	59	.003ᵃ	.036ᵃ	.25ᵃ				1.0			M	
Corn starch	6	1 T			5.4	22					Neutral						A	
Cornstarch, blanc mange	100	1/3c	2.9	3.5	21.0	127	.105	.081	.21				1.6			M	
Corn syrup, (Karo)	100	5T			75.0	300											J	
Corn syrup, (Karo)	40	2T.			30.0	120											J	
Crabmeat, canned	100	2/3c flaked	15.8	1.5	.7	79	.017	.181							80.0	A	A
Crackers, graham²⁵	100	10 crackers	10.0	9.4	72.3	414	.024	.203	1.85				8.5	1.5	5.4	A	B₁
Crackers, graham²⁵	10	1 cracker	1.0	.9	7.2	41	.002	.020	.18				.8	.1	.5	A	B₁
Crackers, saltines	100	13 crackers	10.6	12.7	68.0	429	.022	.102	1.50				8.2	.5	5.6	A	D
Crackers, saltines	8	1 double cracker 4"x2"	.9	1.0	5.4	34	.002	.008	.10				.7		.3	A	D
Crackers, soda	100	36 crackers	9.8	9.1	72.8	412	.022	.102	1.50				8.2	.3	5.9	A	D
Crackers, soda	3	1 cracker 2"x2"	.3	.3	2.2	12	.001	.003	.04				.2		.2	A	D
Cranberries, A.P.	100	1c	.4	.7	9.9	47	.018	.013	.44	*	*	+	.7ᵃ	1.4	87.4	C	A
Cream, 20% "Coffee"	100	½c	2.9	20.0	4.0	208	.097	.086	.2	+++	++	—To+	.6		72.5	L	D
Cream, 20%	15	1 T	.4	3.0	.6	31	.014	.013	.03	+++	++	—To+	.1		10.9	L	D
Cream, 20%	226	1c	6.5	45.2	9.0	470	.219	.194	.55	+,++	++	—To+	1.4		63.8	L	D
Cream, 32% "Whipping"	100	½c	2.4	32.0	3.5	312	.092	.077	.20	+++	++	—To+	.5			F	I

ᵃ Minerals on basis of 50% Graham and Patent flour.

FOOD	Wt. GRAMS	MEASURE	PRO. gms.	FAT gms.	CHO. gms.	CALORIES	Ca. gms.	P. gms	Fe. mgms.	VITAMINS A	B	C	EXCESS Acid	Base	FIBER gms.	WATER gms.	SOURCE	
Cream, 32%	15	1 T	.36	4.8	.53	47	.014	.012	.03	+++	++	—To+		.08			F	I
Cream, 40%	100	—½c	2.2	40.0	3.0	381	.086	.067	.20	+++	++	—To+		.4		54.3	L	D
Cream, 40%	15	1 T	.3	6.0	.4	57	.013	.010	.03	+++	++	—To+		.06		8.1	L	D
Cream, 40%, whipped	10	1 T	.2	4.0	.3	38	.009	.007	.02	+++	++	—To+		.04		.5	L	D
Cress, see Watercress																		
Cucumber	100	1/3c sliced, or 3"x1¼" diam.	.7	.1	2.2	12	.016	.033	.33	—To+	+	++		7.9	.5	96.1	D	A
Currants, dried	100	2/3c	2.4	1.7	74.2[1]	322	.082	.195	3.99					5.8	24.9[18]	17.2	A	A
Currants, fresh	100	½c	1.6	.4	9.5	48	.026	.038	.63					.7[9]	3.2	84.7	C	A
Custard	134	½c	6.3	6.3	16.3	147	.138	.134	.79				.4				M	
Dandelion greens	100	½c cooked	2.7	.7	7.0	44	.105	.072	3.03	++	++	+		27.0[6]	1.8	85.8	D	D
Dates, E. P.	100	14 dates	2.1	2.8	78.4[2]	347	.065	.056	3.56	+	++	•		11.0		15.4	A	A
Doughnuts	45	1 - 3" diam. 1½" thick	3.0	10.0	24.5	200							3.3				M	
Dressing, Meat or Poultry	35	¼c	3.2	6.9	15.2	136	.026	.041	.30				1.7		.1		M	
Duck	100	2 slices 1¾"x1½"x¼" cooked	22.3	3.3		119	.013	.240	1.71	—To+	+	•					F	B_1
Eggs, whole	100	2 med. size eggs	13.4	10.5		148	.067	.180	2.52	++	+To++	•	11.1			73.7	A	B_1
Eggs, whole	50	1 medium	6.7	5.2		74	.033	.090	1.26	++	+To++	•	5.5			36.8	A	B_1
Egg white	100	3 whites	12.3	.2		51	.015	.014	.1	—	—	•	4.8			86.2	A	D
Egg, white	34	1 white	4.2	.1		17	.005	.005	.03	—	—	•	1.6			29.3	A	D
Egg, yolk	100	6 - 7 yolks	15.7	33.3		362	.137	.524	7.60	+++	++	•	25.3			49.5	A	B_1
Egg, yolk	16	1 yolk	2.5	5.3		58	.022	.084	1.22	+++	++	•	4.0			7.9	A	B_1
Eggplant	100	Slice 4½"x½" or 1c diced	1.1	.2	4.6	25	.011	.034	.47	+	+	•			.9	92.7	D	A
Endive	100	2 to 4 stalks or ½ hd.	1.6	.2	3.2	21	.104	.038	1.23	+	•	+		7.4[17]	.8	93.3	D	A
Farina, uncooked	100	⅝c	11.0	1.4	75.9	360	.021	.125	.85	—	—To+	—	9.6		.4	10.9	A	B_1
Farina, cooked	100	½c	1.8	.3	12.4	59	.003	.020	.14				1.6		.1		M	
Figs, fresh[17]	100	3 - 1½" diam.	1.4	.4	17.9	81	.053	.036	.79						1.7	78.0	C	A

[18] Calc. from currants, fresh.
[17] No data available. Figure given is that of lettuce.

FOOD	Wt. GRAMS	MEASURE	PRO. gms.	FAT gms.	CHO. gms.	CALORIES	Ca. gms.	P. gms.	Fe. mgms.	VITAMINS A	VITAMINS B	VITAMINS C	EXCESS Acid	EXCESS Base	FIBER gms.	WATER gms.	SOURCE	
Figs, dried	100	17 figs	4.3	.3	67.5	290	.162	.116	2.87					100.9	6.7	18.8	G	A
Filberts (Hazelnuts)	100	½c	15.6	65.3	13.0³	702				•	++	•			.4	3.7	A	A
Flour, buckwheat	100	¾c	6.4	1.2	77.5	346	.010	.176	3.20				6.9		.4	13.6	A	B₁
Flour, rye	100	¾c	6.8	.9	78.3	349	.018	.289	2.83						.4	12.9	A	B₁
Flour, graham	100	¾c	13.3	2.2	69.5	351	.039	.364	3.70	—			11.2		1.9	11.3	A	B₂
Flour, white, unsifted	100	·¾c	11.2	1.0	74.7	353	.020	.092	.91	—	—To+		9.6		.2	12.4	A	B₂
Flour, white	8	1 T	.9	.1	6.0	28	.002	.007	.07	—	—To+		.8			1.0	A	B₁
Flour, sifted	110	1c	12.3	1.1	82.2	388	.022	.101	1.00	—	—To+		10.6		.2	13.6	A	B₂
Flour, unsifted	125	1c	14.0	1.2	93.4	441	.025	.115	1.14	—	—To+		12.0		.4	15.5	A	B₂
Flour, whole wheat	100	¾c	13.8	1.9	71.0	356	.031	.238	2.5	—	—To+	•	12.2		.9	11.4	A	D
Frankfurters	100	2, 5¾"x1" diam.	19.6	18.6	1.1	250	.011	.216	2.5				10.2			57.2	A	D
Fudge, chocolate	25	1" cube	.5	1.9	18.5	93	.010	.017	.09					.1			M	
Garlic	100	3, 1½" bulbs	4.4	.2	19.0	95									1.0	74.2	D	
Gelatin (dry)	100	10 T	91.4	.1		366										13.6	A	
Gelatin (dry)	3	1 t	2.7			11										.4	A	
Gelatin Dessert (Lemon Jelly)	100	½c	1.6		18.3	80	.002	.001	.02					.5			M	
Gingerale	100	½c			8.0	32											D	
Gingerbread	34	2"x2"x1"	1.7	2.4	15.9	92	.038	.024	1.01					5.8	.1		M	
Goose, young	100		16.3	36.2		391	.009	.176	2.02	—To+	+		7.7			46.7	A	B₁
Gooseberries	100	½c	.8	.4	7.6	37	.035	.031	.48			•			2.5	88.3	C	A
Grapes, American types	100	½c or 24 grapes	1.4	1.4	14.4	76	.019	.031	Pulp .74 Skin 1.36	+	+To+	+		2.7	.5 Pulp .52 whole	81.9	C	B₁
Grapes, European types	100	½c	.8	.4	16.2	72		Malaga 2.28 Red .90	.30		—To++			2.7	.5	81.6	C	B₁
Grape juice, Concord	100	½c	.3		17.3	70	.011	.011	.30	+	+To++	+		3.9		82.1	C	D

FOOD	Wt. GRAMS	MEASURE	PRO. gms.	FAT gms.	CHO. gms.	CALORIES	Ca. gms.	P. gms.	Fe. mgms.	VITAMINS A	VITAMINS B	VITAMINS C	EXCESS Acid	EXCESS Base	FIBER gms.	WATER gms.	SOURCE	
Grape juice, Catawba	100	—½c	.4	.2	20.2	82								3.9		79.1	C	A
Grapefruit, E.P.	100[19]	½ · 4" diam. or ½c	.5	.2	9.8	43	.021	.020	.27	+	++	+++		5.6[18]	.3	88.8	C	A
Grapefruit Juice	100	—⅜c			6.7	27										89.9	C	
Gravy, meat stock[20]	100	⅜c	.7	9.0	4.5	102	.003	.006	.07				.6					
Gravy, meat stock	15	1 T	.1	1.3	.6	14		.001	.01				.1					
Halibut	100	4"x1¼"x¾"	18.6	5.2		121	.020	.214	.93	—To+	+	•	9.4			75.4	A	B_1
Ham, boiled	100	2 sl. 4½"x4½"x⅛"	20.2	22.4		282	.012	.218	1.7[21]	—To+	++	—	10.0			51.3	A	C
Ham, fresh, lean	100	4½"x3"x¼"	25.0	14.4		230	.014	.269	2.1[21]	—To+	++	—	12.5			60.0	A	C
Ham, smoked, med. fat	100	4½"x4½"x¼"	16.3	38.8		414	.009	.176	1.4	—To+	++	—	8.3			40.3	A	C
Hash	113	½c	16.3	20.8	12.8	304	.019	.200	3.84				2.9		.3		M	
Hazelnuts (filberts)	100	½c	15.6	65.3	13.0[1]	702	.287	.354	4.50							3.7	A	B_1
Heart, beef	100	2"x3"x1"	16.0	20.4		248	.009	.172	4.8	++[22]	++[22]	+[22]	9.1			62.6	A	B_2
Hickory nuts	100	½c chopped	15.4	67.4	11.4[1]	714			2.38	•	++	•				3.7	A	B_1
Hermits	10	1 cookie 2" diam.	[illegible]	.5	6.3	41	.003	.007	.12				.3				M	
Hominy, cooked	100	½c	2.2	.2	17.8	82	.002[3]	.020[3]	.10[3]						.2[3]		A	
Hominy, uncooked	100	½c	8.3	.6	78.1	351	.011	.144	.54						.9	11.8	A	B_1
Honey	100	5 T	[illegible]		81.2	326	.004	.019	1.15	—	—	—				18.2	A	B_1
Honeydew, A. P.	100	" wedge from 7" melon	.4	.1	3.7	18												
Huckleberries, see Blueberries																		
Ice Cream, vanilla	100	⅝c	2.5	17.1	18.2	237	.082	.080	.21					.5			M	
Jelly	100	5 T	1.0		77.2	313	.014	.008	.30							21.0	A	D
Jelly, (see Gelatin dessert)																		
Kale	100	1c cooked	3.9	.6	6.0	45			2.54	++	•	•			1.2	86.6	D	A
Kidney, beef	100		15.0	8.0		142	.009	.162	5.50	++[22]	++[22]	+[22]				76.7	B	C

[18] No data available. Figure given is that of oranges.
[19] Average A. P. wt. 150 gms.
[20] 2 T. Fat. 2 T. Flour per cup stock.
[21] Calculated from Smoked Ham.
[22] Values given are those of Pork Heart.

FOOD	Wt. GRAMS	MEASURE	PRO. gms.	FAT gms.	CHO. gms.	CALORIES	Ca. gms.	P. gms.	Fe. mgms.	VITAMINS A	VITAMINS B	VITAMINS C	EXCESS Acid	EXCESS Base	FIBER gms.	WATER gms.	SOURCE	
Kidney, veal	100	½c diced	16.9	6.4		125	.010	.182	4.0	++[23]	++[23]	+[23]	8.4			75.8	A	C
Kohlrabi	100	½c diced	2.1	.1	5.6	32	.077	.071	.61	•	•	+			1.1	90.1	D	A
Lamb, chops, E.P.	100	3 med. size chops	18.7	28.3		329	.011	.202	1.6	—To+	+	•	9.3			53.1	A	C
Lamb, chops, A.P.	100	2 med. sized chops	16.0	24.1		281	.009	.172	1.4	—To+	+	•	8.0			45.3	A	C
Lamb, roast	100	slice 4½"x5"x¼"	19.7	12.7		193	.011	.212	1.7	—To+	+	•	10.7			67.1	A	C
Lard	14	1 T		14.0		126				—To+	—	—	Neutral				A	A
Leeks	100	1c ½" pieces	2.5	.4	6.6	40	.058	.006	.65						1.3	88.2	D	A
Lemons, A.P.	100	1 lemon, 2¾" long	.6	.4	4.8	25	.019	.026	.4	+	++	+++		3.3	.6	55.4	C	D
Lemons, E.P.	100		.9	.6	7.8	40	.030	.042	.60	+	++	+++		5.5	.9	89.3	C	D
Lemon juice	100	½c			8.3	33	.024	.010	.15	+	++	+++		4.1		89.4	C	B_1
Lemon juice	15	1 T			1.2	5	.004	.001		+	++	+++		.7		13.4	C	B_1
Lentils, dry	100	3c	25.7	1.0	59.2[1]	349	.107	.438	8.6	+	++	—	5.2			8.4	A	D
Lettuce	100	6 leaves of leaf, or 8 of head, or ¼ 4" head + 1 leaf	1.2	.2	2.3	16	.043	.042	Head .42 Leaf 1.87	+To++ +++	++ • ++	+++ +++		7.4	.6	94.8	D	B_1
Limes, sweet	100	2-1¾" long	.8	.1	8.6	56	.055	.036		—	•	++		5.3[24]	.3	89.6	C	B_1
Lime juice	100	—½c	.5		7.8	33				—	•	++				91.3	C	B_1
Liver, beef, uncooked	100	3"x6"x½"	20.4	4.5	1.7	129	.012	.220	8.3	++ To+++	++	•	10.1			71.2	A	B_1
Liver, calves, uncooked	100	3"x6"x½"	19.0	5.3		124	.011	.205	5.4	++ To+++	++	•	.94			73.0	A	B_1
Lobster	100	2/3c flaked	18.1	1.1	.5	84	.020	.208	.44	—To+	+	•				77.8	A	B_1
Logan-berries[27]	100	1 1/6c	1.0	.6	13.6	64									1.4	82.9	C	
Macaroni and cheese	100	⅞c	5.7	7.5	13.8	146	.114	.116	.40					2.1			M	
Macaroni, cooked	100	+½c	3.0	1.5	15.8	89	.005[3]	.032[3]	.26[3]				1.7[3]				A	
Macaroni, uncooked	100	1c	13.4	.9	74.1	358	.022	.144	1.2				9.6			10.3	A	D
Mackerel	100	2"x3"x1" •	18.7	7.1		139	.020	.215	.75	+	+	•	9.3			73.4	A	B_1

[23] Values given are those of Pork Kidney.
[24] No data available. Figure that of lemons.
[28] Made to approximate the composition of butter, for convenience in diet calculation. Contains 1 Egg, 2 C. Salad Oil, 2 T. Vinegar, 1 t. Salt, 1 t. Mustard, ¼ t. Pepper.

FOOD	Wt. GRAMS	MEASURE	PRO. gms.	FAT gms.	CHO. gms.	CALO-RIES	Ca. gms.	P. gms.	Fe. mgms.	VITAMINS A	VITAMINS B	VITAMINS C	EXCESS Acid	EXCESS Base	FIBER gms.	WATER gms.	SOURCE	SOURCE
Marmalade, Orange	30	1 1/3 T.	.2		25.3	102								.3			F	A
Marshmallows	100	13	1.9		80.1	328										18.0	J	
Mayonnaise	100	1/2c	1.1	74.8	2.5	687	.012	.037	.53				1.4				M	
Mayonnaise	15	1 T	.2	11.2	.4	103	.002	.006	.08				.2				M	
Mayonnaise dressing, special	100	1/2c	1.3	83.4		756	.007	.018	.25				1.1					
Milk, whole	100	3/8c	3.3	4.0	5.0	69	.120	.093	.24	+++	++	—To+		1.8		87.0	A	B₁
Milk, whole	200	3/4c or 1 glass	6.6	8.0	10.0	138	.240	.186	.48	+++	++	—To+		3.6		174.0	A	B₁
Milk, whole	240	1c	7.9	9.6	12.0	166	.288	.223	.58	+++	++	—To+		4.3		208.8	A	B₁
Milk, skim	100	1/2c	3.4	.3	5.1	37	.122	.096	.25	+	++	—To+		1.8		90.5	A	D
Milk, condensed, sweetened	100	1/3c	8.8	8.3	54.1	326	.300	.233	.60	+++	++	+		4.5		26.9	A	D
Milk, evaporated[2a]	100	1/3c	9.6	9.3	11.2	167	.349	.271	.7	+++	++	—To+		4.6		68.2	A	B₁
Milk, malted, dry	100	3/4c	13.8	6.8	71.9	404				T+++	To+++						E	
Milk, malted, dry	12	1 T	1.7	.8	8.6	48	.028	.014									E	
Milk, Mothers	100c	1/2c	1.0	4.5	7.0	72				++	—To+	+					Q	
Milk, Top, 8 oz.	100	3/8c	3.0	14.0	4.3	155	.108	.089	.22		—To+	—		1.2			F	
Molasses	100	3 1/2 T	2.4		69.3	287	.211	.044	7.97	—	+	—		59.4		25.1	A	B₁
Molasses	280	1c	6.7		194.0	803	.591	.123	22.32	—	+	—		166.3		70.3	A	B₁
Muffins (1 Egg)	47	1 muffin	3.9	4.1	20.2	134	.037	.053	.39	•	•	+	2.2		.1		M	
Mulberries	100	2/3c	1.2	.6	12.6	61				•	•				2.0	82.8	C	A
Mushrooms[2a]	100	1/2c (cooked)	2.3	.3			.017	.108	.73	—To+		—		3.9	.9	91.1	C	A
Mustard greens	100	1/2c cooked	2.3	.3	3.2	25			2.87						.8	92.2	D	A
Noodles, uncooked	100	1 2/3c	11.7	1.0	75.2	357									.4	10.7	D	A
Noodles, cooked	100	1/2c	2.6	.2	16.8	80									.1		A	
Oatmeal, rolled oats, unckd.	100	1 1/3c	16.1	7.2	66.6	396	.069	.392	3.80	—To+	++	—	12.0		.9	7.7	A	B₁
Oatmeal, cooked	100	1/2c scant	2.7	1.2	11.1	66	.011[a]	.065[a]	.63[a]				2.0		.1		A	

2a Minerals calculated from whole milk.
b J. of Home Ec. 22:123 (1930).

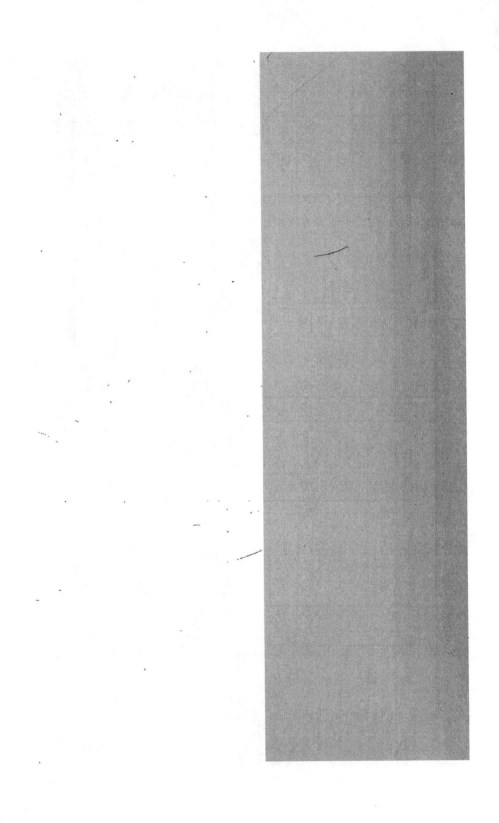

FOOD	Wt. GRAMS	MEASURE	PRO. gms.	FAT gms.	CHO. gms.	CALORIES	Ca. gms.	P. gms.	Fe. mgms.	VITAMINS A	VITAMINS B	VITAMINS C	EXCESS Acid Base	FIBER gms.	WATER gms.	*OTHER*	
Oil, olive or salad	206	1c	206.0			854				-To+			Neutral			F	A
Oil, olive or salad	14	1 T	14.0			126				-To+			Neutral			F	A
Oleomargerine	100	7Tb.	83.0			752				-To++²⁰	-	-			9.5	A	A
Oleomargerine	14	1 T	11.6			105	.1			-To++²⁰	-	-			1.3	A	A
Olives, green plain, A.P.	100	13 olives, 1¼"x¾"	.8	20.2	8.5¹	219	.122	.014	2.11				41.1		42.3	A	B₁
Olives, ripe, A.P.	100	20 Med. Size	1.4	21.0	3.5¹	209									52.4	A	A
Okra	100	½c canned	1.8	.2	6.4	35	.071	.019	.63	*	++	*		1.0	89.8	D	A
Onions	100	½c or 3, 1½" diam.	1.4	.2	9.5	45	.031	.045	.48	-To+	+	+cooked ++raw	1.5	.8	87.5	D	A
Onions, young green	100	20, 5" long	1.0	.2	8.8	41			.47	-To+	+	++		1.8	87.6	D	A
Oranges, E.P.	100²⁰	Pulp of orange 2½" diam.	.9	.2	10.6	48	.045	.021	.52	*	*	+++	5.6	.6	87.2	C	A
Orange Juice	100	½c	.6		9.1	39	.029	.016	.24	*To-+	++	+++	4.5		85.7	C	A
Oysters	100	1/3c standards	6.2	1.2	3.7	50	.052	.155	3.14	Raw++ Cooked*	++ +	+ *	15.2		86.9	A	B₁
Oyster plant (see Vegetable Oyster)																	
Papayas	100		.6	.1	9.1	40				++	+	+++		.9	88.7	C	A
Parsley	100	bunch 5" diam.	3.7	1.0	7.2	53			3.16	*	++	*		1.8	83.9	D	A
Parsnips	100	½c diced	1.5	.5	16.0	74	.059	.076	.77	-To+	++	*	11.9	2.2	78.6	A	A
Pastry, plain	90 uncooked 80 cooked	one 9" crust	5.3	26.4	34.1	396	.011	.044	.44				4.4	.1		M	
Papaws	100		5.2	.9	16.8	96									76.6	C	
Peaches, fresh²²	100	1 medium	.5	.1	11.4	48	.016	.024	.33	+To++	+	++	5.0	.6	86.9	C	A
Peanuts	100	¾c	25.8	38.6	21.9	538	.071	.399	2.31	+	++			2.5	9.2	A	B₁
Peanut butter²¹	100	6 T	29.3	46.5	17.1¹	604	.080	.451	2.6	+	++	*	3.9			A	B₁
Peanut butter²¹	16	1 T	4.7	7.4	2.7¹	97	.013	.072	.4	+	++	*	4.4			A	B₁
Pears, fresh²³	100	1 medium	.7	.4	14.4	64	.015	.026	.32	* +To++	+	+	3.6	1.4	82.7	A	C

²⁰ Vitamins A and D vary with method of manufacture. Nucoa contains amounts comparable to butter.
²¹ protein content low. Nitrogen mainly as Non-Protein Nitrogen. Carbohydrate mostly non-extractible, presumably of no nutritive value.
²² Average A. P. wt. 139 gm.
²³ Minerals calculated from peanuts E. P.

FOOD	Wt. GRAMS	MEASURE	PRO. gms.	FAT gms.	CHO. gms.	CALORIES	Ca. gms.	P. gms.	Fe. mgms.	VITAMINS A	VITAMINS B	VITAMINS C	EXCESS Acid	EXCESS Base	FIBER gms.	WATER gms.	SOURCE	
Peas, fresh	100	¾c	6.7	.4	15.5	92	.028	.127	2.07	++	++	+++		1.3	2.2	74.3	D	A
Peas, dried	100	½c	24.6	1.0	57.5	337	.084	.400	5.7	+	++	•		5.4	4.5	9.5	A	D
Peas, canned, incl. liquor	150	¾c	5.2	.5	12.9	77	.027[3]	.122[3]	2.05[3]	++	+To++	++		1.3	1.8		K	A
Peas, canned, drained	100	⅝c	4.6	.5	11.2	68				++	+To++	++			1.8		K	A
Peas, canned, liquor only	100	—½c	1.5		4.0	22											K	
Pea, cream of, see Soup																		
Pecans	100	⅞c	11.0	71.2	13.3[1]	738	.089	.335	2.58	+	++	•				3.0	A	B_1
Peppers, green	100	1, 3⅝" long	1.2	.2	4.3	24	.006	.026	.40	++	++	+++			1.4	92.4	D	A
Peppers, red	100	½c	1.3	.7	6.5	37			.60						1.6	89.2	D	B_1
Pie, apple	134	1/6 of pie 9" diam.	2.1	9.2	42.8	262	.011	.026	.46					2.2	1.0		M	
Pie, cream	122	1/6 of pie 9" diam.	6.5	9.4	32.2	239	.110	.118	.75				1.8				M	
Pineapple, fresh[87]	100	½c diced or 2 slices 3½"x⅜"	.4	.2	13.3	57	.018	.028	.37	++	++	++		6.8	.4	85.3	C	A
Pistachio nuts	100	2/3c	22.3	54.0	16.3	640			7.92						1.8	4.2	A	B_1
Plums, fresh[87]	100	3 - 1½" diam.	.7	.2	12.4	54	.020	.032	.56	•	++	•	?[4]		.5	85.7	C	A
Pomegranates	100		1.5	1.2	17.3	86	.011	.105	.78						3.6		C	A
Popcorn, popped	100	9c	10.7	5.0	77.3	397									1.4	4.3	A	
Popcorn, popped	11	1c	1.2	.5	8.5	43										.5	A	
Pork chops, lean	100	1 med. chop ½" thick	20.3	19.0		252	.012	.219	1.5	—To+	++	•	10.0			60.3	A	C
Pork chops, med. fat	100	1 med. chop ½" thick	16.6	30.1		337	.010	.179	1.3	—To+	++	•	8.3			52.0	A	C
Pork sausage	100	7 —3"x¾"	13.0	44.2	1.1	454	.008	.140	1.0	—To+	++	•	6.4			39.8	A	C
Potato, white, raw or steamed	100	one 2½" diam. or ⅝c diced	2.0	.1	18.7	84	.014	.058	.85	+	++	++		7.0	.4	77.8	D	B_1
Potatoes, white, baked	67[14]	one 2½" diam.	2.0	.1	18.7	84	.014	.058	.85	+	++	+To++		7.0	.4	44.8		
Potato, white, mashed	100	½c	2.0	6.4	15.7	129	.028	.060	.73					6.0	.3		M	
Potato, white, creamed	100	½c	2.9	5.9	14.7	124	.060	.075	.61					4.5	.2		M	
Potato, white, fried[82]	100	—½c	2.1	8.6	18.7	161	.015	.060	.87					7.2	.4			

[82] Potato 100 gms., Fat 10 gms.

FOOD	WT. GRAMS	MEASURE	PRO. gms.	FAT gms.	CHO. gms.	CALORIES	Ca. gms.	P. gms.	Fe. mgms.	VITAMINS A	VITAMINS B	VITAMINS C	EXCESS Acid	EXCESS Base	FIBER gms.	WATER gms.	SOURCE	SOURCE
Potato chips	20	10 to 12 large chips.	1.4	8.0	9.3[1]	115		.052					3.6		.4	.4	A	A
Potato salad	100	1 leaf lettuce + ½c salad	1.7	11.1	13.6	163	.018	.052	.74					6.0	.4		A	M
Potato, sweet, uncooked	100	½ med. size	1.8	.7	26.9	121	.019	.045	.77	+To++	++	++		6.7	1.0	68.5	A	A
Potato, sweet, baked	85[14]	¼ med. size	1.8	.7	26.9	121	.019	.045	.77	+To++	•	•		6.7	1.3			
Prunes, fresh[27]	100	3 – 1½" diam.	.9	.2	21.3	91				•	•	•	7*		.5	76.5	C	C
Prunes, dried, A.P.	100	12 prunes 50/60s	2.1	.2	73.3[2]	302	.054	.105	2.85	++	++	–	7*		2.4		A	A
Prunes, dried, cooked A.P.	100	3 prunes + 3 T juice	.6		34.2	139	.015	.030	.81	•	•	•	7*		.7		A	M
Puffed rice	10	½c	.8		7.9	35	.001	.010	.11				.9		.01		B₁	E
Puffed wheat	10	½c	1.3	.2	7.0	35	.004	.042	.41				1.1		.2		B₁	E
Pumpkin	100	½c cooked	1.2	.2	6.0	31	.023	.059	.93	++	•	•		1.5	1.3	90.5	A	A
Quinces	100	3 - 1½" diam.	.3	.1	12.1	50			1.01						1.8	85.3	B₁	C
Radishes	100	10 - 1" diam.	1.2	.1	3.5	18	.021	.029	.83	–	++	++		2.9	.7	93.6	A	A
Raisins	100	¾c	2.6	3.3	76.1[2]	344	.064	.132	Seeded 5.69 Seedless 2.99	–	+	–	23.7		.65 / 1.5	14.6	A / A	A / A
Raspberries, black, fresh[37]	100	1 1/6c	1.5	1.6	12.1	69	.049	.052	.99	•	•	++			3.5	80.7	B₁	C
Raspberries, red, fresh[38]	100	1c	1.1	.6	11.6	56	.049	.052	.99	•	•	++			2.8	83.4	B₁	C
Rhubarb, fresh	100	—½c cooked	.5	.1	3.1	15	.044	.031	.56	•	•	+		8.6	.7	94.9	A	C
Rice Krispies	100	3½c	6.0	.3	88.4	380	.011	.010	2.7						.3	1.9	A	J
Rice, polished, uncooked	100	½c	8.0	.3	78.8	350	.009	.096	1.05	–	–	–	9.3		.2	12.3	B₁	A
Rice, polished, cooked	100	½c	1.8	.1	21.3	93	.002[3]	.026[3]	.28[3]	–	–	–	2.5		.1		F	A
Rice, brown, uncooked	100	½c						.207	2.0	+	++	–	9.3[33]				D	D
Rice pudding	88	½c	4.3	3.6	12.0	98												M[3]
Romaine	100	1/3 large head	No data available. See figures for lettuce				.045	.053		++	++	•						A
Rutabagas	100	½c mashed	1.1	.1	7.6	36	.074	.056	.36	+	++	+++[33]		8.5	1.3	89.1	D	A
Salad Dressing, Boiled	100	⅛ or 5 T	3.6	10.9	11.2	157	.080	.102	.86				1.9				D	M

** No data available. Figure is that of Polished rice.
** Rutabagas, cold storage, vitamin C. ++.

FOOD	WT. GRAMS	MEASURE	P₂O₅ gms.	FAT gms.	CHO. gms.	calories	Ca. gms.	P. gms.	Fe. mgms.	VITAMINS A	VITAMINS B	VITAMINS C	EXCESS Acid	EXCESS Base	FIBER gms.	WATER gms.	source	source
French Dressing	13	1 T		7.3		60												M
Mayonnaise, see Mayonnaise Dressing																		
Salmon, fresh	100	3"x4"x¾"	22.0	12.8		203	.024	.253	.83	+	+	•	11.0			64.6	A	B₁
Salmon, canned	100	¾c flaked	21.8	12.1		196	.024	.250		+	•	•	10.8			63.5	A	B₁
Salsify—See Vegetable Oyster																		
Sardines	100	4-3½" long	23.0	19.7		269	.025	.264	1.3				11.4			52.3	A	D
Sauerkraut	100	2/3c	1.7	.5	3.8*	27	.041	.324		+	+	+To+++		5.7*			A	A
Shredded wheat	100	3 1/3 biscuits	10.5	1.4	76.2	359	.041	.324	4.5				12.2		1.7	8.1	A	D
Shredded wheat	28	1 biscuit	2.9	.4	21.3	101	.011	.091	1...				3.4		.5	1.5	A	D
Shrimp, canned	100	½c	25.4	1.0	.2	111	.028	.292	2.67	+	•	•				70.8	A	B₁
Soup, vegetable (Julienne)	218	1c	4.7	.2	2.5	31	.016	.013	.19					1.5	.3			N
Soup, cream of pea	100	⅜c	2.8	3.3	6.1	64	.050	.070	.34**					.9	.6			M
Soup, cream of tomato	100	½c	3.0	7.7	7.1	109	.090	.076	.38					2.7	.2			M
Spaghetti, cooked*	100	½c	2.7	.1	16.9	80	.005	.032	.47				2.1		.1			
Spaghetti, uncooked	100	¾c	12.1	.4	75.9	356	.022	.144	1.25				9.6		.4	10.6	A	D
Spinach	100	½c cooked	2.3	.3	2.6	22	.067	.068	2.55	+++	+†**	+++**		27.0	.6	92.7	D	A
Squash, summer	100	½c cooked	.6	.1	3.4	17	.018		.35						.5	95.0	D	A
Squash, winter	100	½c mashed	1.5	.3	7.4	38	.018		.55	++	•	•		2.8	1.4	88.6	D	A
Starch, corn	100	¾c			90.0	360								Neutral			A	E
Strawberries, fresh**	100	2/3c	.8	.6	6.9	36	.041	.028	.68	+	+	+++			1.2	90.0	C	A
Sugar, granulated	100	½c scant			100.0	400				-	-	-		Neutral			A	A
Sugar, granulated	4	1 t			4.0	16												A
Sugar, granulated	13	1 T			13.0	52												A
Sugar, granulated	210	1c			210.0	840												A
Sugar, powdered	100	½c			100.0	400												A
Sugar, powdered	12	1 T			12.0	48												A

** Spinach, canned or cooked, vitamin B +, vitamin C, + to ++.
** Estimates a loss of 2/3 Fe content in straining.

[14]

FOOD	Wt. GRAMS	MEASURE	PRO. gms.	FAT gms.	CHO. gms.	CALORIES	Ca. gms.	P. gms.	Fe. mgms.	VITAMINS A	B	C	EXCESS Acid	Base	FIBER gms.	WATER gms.	SOURCE	
Sugar, powdered	170	1c			170.0	680											A	
Sugar, brown	10	1 T			9.5	38											A	
Sugar, brown	165	1c			156.7	627											A	
Summer Sausage, E. P.	100	4 Sl. 3"x⅛"	26.0	44.5		504											A	
Sweetbreads	100	2½"x3"x¾"	16.8	12.1		176				+	+	•				70.9	A	B_1
Tangerines, Mandarin oranges	100	2 - 2" diam.	.8	.3	9.9	45			.61	•	•	+++		5.6[17]	1.0	87.3	C	B_1
Tapioca, uncooked	184	1c	.7	.2	161.7	651	.042	.166	2.94						.2	21.0	A	D
Tapioca, uncooked	100	+½c - 9 Tb.	.4	.1	87.9	354	.023	.090	1.6					Neutral	.1	11.4	A	D
Tapioca, cooked[2]	100	1/3c	.1		13.7	55	.004	.014	.25								A	D
Tapioca, apple	100	½c	.2	.3	27.5	113	.006	.016	.35					2.2	.6		M	
Tapioca, cream	100	½c	3.6	3.9	17.1	118	.090	.091	.48					.5			M	
Tomato, raw, A.P.	100	One 2½" diam. or ⅜c canned	1.0	.3	3.4	20	.011	.026	.44	++	++	+++[18]		5.6	.6	94.1	D	A
Tomato soup, canned	100	1/3c	1.5	.7	9.5	50			2.20	++	++ To+++						F	B_1
Tomato, cream of, see Soup																		
Trout	100	2"x3"x1"	17.8	10.3		164	.019	.204	.78	+	+	•	8.9			70.8	A	B_1
Tunafish (Tunney) in oil	100	½c flaked	23.8	20.0		275	.026	.263	1.31							51.3	A	B_1
Turkey, dark meat, cooked	100	4 slices 1¼"x1½"x⅛"	39.2	4.3		195	.023	.423		—To+	+	•	19.3				F	A
Turkey, dark meat, unckd.	100		21.4	20.6		271	.012	.231	2.04	—To+	+	•	10.4				F	B_1
Turkey, light meat, cooked	100	2 slices 3½"x3"x¼"	34.6	4.9		182	.020	.373		—To+	+	•	17.1				F	A
Turkey, light meat, unckd.	100		25.7	9.4		187	.015	.277	1.03	—To+	+	•	12.7				F	B_1
Turnips	100	½c cooked	1.1	.2	6.0	30	.064	.046	.52	—To+	++	++		2.7	1.1	90.9	A	A
Turnip tops	100	½c cooked	2.9	.4	4.2	32	.347	.049	3.48	+++	++	—To+			1.2	89.5	F	A
Veal chop, med. fat	100	1 med. size ⅜" thick	19.9	10.8		177	.012	.215	2.7	—To+	+	•	9.8			69.0	A	C
Veal roast	100	3"x2¼"x¼"	26.6	4.8		150	.015	.287	3.6	—To+	+	•	13.0				M	C

[18] Canned Tomatoes, Vit. C ++ to +++.

FOOD	Wt. GRAMS	MEASURE	PRO. gms.	FAT gms.	CHO. gms.	CALORIES	Ca. gms.	P. gms.	Fe. mgms.	VITAMINS A	VITAMINS B	VITAMINS C	EXCESS Acid	EXCESS Base	FIBER gms.	WATER gms.	SOURCE	
Vegetable oyster, Salsify	100	½c diced	3.5	1.0	13.7[20]	70			1.60						1.8	79.1	D	A
Vegetables, 5%	100	± ½c	1.0		5.0	24	see pp. 12 for mineral, vitamin, base and											
Vegetables and fruits, 10%	100	± ½c	1.0		10.0	44	fiber values, see figures for individual foods.											
Vegetables and fruits, 15%	100	± ½c	1.0		14.0	60												
Vegetables and fruits, 20%	100	± ½c	1.0		20.0	84												
Waffles	64	1 waffle 6" diam.	8.8	8.5	31.6	239	.072	.116	1.07				5.6		.1		M	
Waldorf salad	162	1 leaf lettuce + ½c salad	2.0	17.8	14.9	225	.047	.055	.82					6.5	1.1		M	
Walnuts, black	100	1 1/6c chopped	27.6	56.3	10.0	657			5.98	•	++	•			1.7	2.5	A	E
Walnuts, English	100	1 1/6c	18.4	64.4	11.6	700	.089	.358	2.14	+	++	•	7.9		1.4	2.5	A	B_1
Watercress	100	40 sprigs - 3c	1.7	.3	2.8	46	.187	.005	2.97	+++	•	+++			.5	83.6	D	A
Watermelon	100	2½"x2½"x1"	.5	.2	6.3	29	.011	.003	.23					2.7	.6	92.1	C	B_1
Whey	100	⅓c	1.0	.3	5.0	27	.044	.035						←		93.0	A	A
Whitefish	100	2"x3"x1"	22.9	6.5		150	.150	.263	.42	—To+	+	•	11.3			69.8	A	B_1
White sauce, medium	100	+1/3c	3.6	12.0	8.6	156	.105	.121	2.8					.9			M	
Yeast, compressed, A.P.	15	1 cake	1.7	.1	3.1	20			.28[20]	—To+	++To +++	•				65.1	A	A
Zwiebach	100	12 pieces 3¼"x1¼"x½"	9.8	9.9	73.5[1]	422											A	

[20] Analysis furnished by M. Winters, University Hospital.

[21] The nutritive value of canned fruits may be estimated as that of the fresh food, plus the carbohydrate and calorie value of the syrup in which it is canned. The weight of the syrup is usually 50-100% of the weight of the drained fruit. The following additions, per 100 gms. of fresh food are an approximation* of the minimum value of these syrups.

	Wt.	Measure	CHO.	Cal.
For fancy grades	60 gms.	¼c.	24.0	96
For choice grades	60 gms.	¼c.	15.0	60
For standard grades	60 gms.	¼c.	9.0	36

*These vary widely with the individual fruit and packer. For example, the syrup used for "fancy" pears and blackberries is approximately the usual concentration used for "choice grades. For details see "How to Buy Canned Foods" National Canners Association, Washington, D. C.

CLASSIFICATION OF FRUITS AND VEGETABLES

(According to Carbohydrate Content)

5% Vegetables	10% Vegetables	15% Vegetables	20% Vegetables
Asparagus	Beets	Artichokes—Globe	Beans—cooked
Bean Sprouts	Brussels Sprouts	Oyster Plant	Kidney
Broccoli	Carrots	Parsnips	Lima
Cabbage	Dandelion Greens	Peas	Navy
Cauliflower	Leeks		Corn
Celery	Olives—green		Horse Radish
Chard	Onions	*15% Fruit*	Potatoes
Chinese Cabbage	Rutabagas	Apples	
Cucumber	Winter Squash	Apricots	*20% Fruit*
Egg Plant		Blueberries	Bananas
Endive	*10% Fruit*	Cherries—sour	Cherries—sweet
Greens—beet	Blackberries	Grapes	Figs—fresh
Greens—mustard	Cranberries	Huckleberries	Grape Juice
Kohlrabi	Currants	Loganberries	Prunes—fresh
Lettuce	Gooseberries	Mulberries	
Okra	Grapefruit	Pears	
Olives—ripe	Lime juice	Pineapple	
Peppers	Oranges	Plums	
Pumpkin	Orange Juice	Raspberries	
Radish	Peaches		
Spinach	Tangerines		
String Beans	Lemon Juice		
Summer Squash			
Tomatoes			
Turnips			
Watercress			
5% Fruit			
Avocado			
Honey Dew Melon			
Muskmelon			
Rhubarb			
Strawberries			
Watermelon			

CEREAL PRODUCTS

10 grams of Dry Cereal, Macaroni, Spaghetti or Noodles is equal to 100 grams of any 10% Fruit or Vegetable

100 grms. 5% Veg. = 50 grms. 10% Veg. = 33 grms. 15% Veg. = 25 grms. 20% Veg.
100 grms. 10% Veg. = 200 grms. 5% Veg. = 70 grms. 15% Veg. = 50 grms. 20% Veg.
100 grms. 15% Veg. = 280 grms. 5% Veg. = 140 grms. 10% Veg. = 70 grms. 20% Veg.
100 grms. 20% Veg. = 400 grms. 5% Veg. = 200 grms. 10% Veg. = 140 grms. 15% Veg.

KEY TO SOURCES OF DATA QUOTED

First letter indicates the source of the data for Protein, Fat, Carbohydrate, Fiber, Water.

Second letter indicates the source of data for Minerals, Vitamins, and Acid-Base preponderance.

First Letter

A—Bulletin 28. U. S. Dept. of Agriculture (1905) "Chemical Composition of American Food Materials".

B—Circular 389. U. S. Dept. of Agriculture (1926) "Proximate Composition of Beef".

C—Circular 50. U. S. Dept. of Agriculture (1928), "Proximate Composition of Fresh Fruits".

D—Circular 146. U. S. Dept. of Agriculture (1931) "Proximate Composition of Fresh Vegetables".

E—Bulletin 286. Connecticut Agricultural Experiment Station "31st Report on Food Products" (1927)

F—"Laboratory Handbook for Dietetics" Mary S. Rose.

G—As under "A" except that Fiber is taken from "The Iron Fiber in Food" Magers, J. Am. Dietetic Ass. 1:173 (1925)

H—As under "C" except Fiber is taken from Magers.

Second Letter

A—Calcium, Phosphorus from "Chemistry of Food and Nutrition" H. C. Sherman.
Iron—"Iron Content of Vegetables and Fruits" Hazel Stiebling, U. S. Dept. of Agriculture Circular No. 205 (1932)
Vitamins A, B, C "Vitamins in Food Materials" Smith, Circular 84 U. S. Dept. of Agriculture.
Acid-Base. "Food Products" H. C. Sherman (1928) and (1916)

B—"Iron Content of Plant and Animal Foods" Peterson and Elvehjem J. B. C. 78:215 (1928)

B—As under "A" except that Iron figure is from "The Iron Content of Animal Tissues" Elvehjem and Peterson, J. B. C. 74.433 (1927)

C—As under "A" except that Iron is from "The Iron Content of Meats" Forbes and Swift J. B. C. 67:517 (1926)

D—As under "A" except that Iron is from "Chemistry of Food and Nutrition" Sherman.

E—As under "A" except that Vitamins A B C values are from "Chemistry of Food and Nutrition" Sherman.

F—As under "A" except that Ca value is from "Calcium of Cheese" Blunt and Summer J. of Home Ec. 20:587 (1928)

G—Minerals from "Laboratory Handbook of Dietetics" M. S. Rose.

H—Minerals from "Food Products" H. C. Sherman

I—Compiler's calculation.

J—Manufacturers analysis.

K—Protein, Fat, Carbohydrate from Connecticut Agricultural Station Report for 1910.

L—"Fundamentals of Dairy Science" Associates of L. A. Rogers.

M—Recipe from "Feeding the Family," Mary S. Rose.

N—Recipe from Boston Cooking School Cook Book.

P—"Food Values and Measures", Stern, Reyner and Barden, Food Clinic of the Boston Dispensary.

Q—Macy et al at Am. J. Dis. Children 43:40 (1932) et ante.

R—Circular 494, U. S. Dept. of Agriculture (1933) "Nutritive Value of Soybeans."

S—U.S. Dept. Agri. Bureau of Home Economics 569 (5/5/34) C.C. Food Composition.